CANTERBURY

8.00 a.m. on the 16th October 1987, and the winds continue bend the surviving trees along the Causeway.

3.   Further along the Causeway, and the way is blocked. The sun rising from behind the Cathedral illuminates the scene.

4.   This warehouse at the end of Holters Lane partially collapsed as dawn broke on the fateful day. Sections of the roof can be seen alongside the railway line.

5. 10.30 a.m. and by now the sun is casting strong shadows from the buildings along Pound Lane, where these trees came down.

6. The Causeway once more, where this fallen tree has distorted an old style electric lamp standard.

7. By mid-morning the winds had dropped considerably, and the clearing up operation, no small task, could begin.

Millers Field is a triangular island, ordered on every side by the River Stour. This view looking towards Pound Lane dates from April 1987. The trunks of some fourteen trees can be counted.

9. A scene of utter devastation across Millers Field, with just one tree standing, in this view from the Causeway.

Millers Field April 1988, taken from same spot as photograph 8. Only ten trees can now be counted.

11. On the three sides of Millers Field are North Lane and the Stour, the Causeway and the Stour, and the relief channel running parallel to Pound Lane. The relief channel is seen here taken in the summer of 1987.

12. On the day of the Hurricane, looking across the same sluice gate where fallen branches are beginning to accumulate.

13. April 1988. This more open scene contrasts with the leaf enclosed view which existed before the Hurricane, as remembered in photograph 11.

St Dunstan's Church. This brick-built chapel carries the me of the Roper family. A large section of it has broken away d smashed a number of monuments on the ground below.

5 & 16. The same church, and the wind-distorted weather-ane hangs over the edge of the tower. A portion of it, however, already at the base of the tower.

17. This old building can be found just off Tower Way. The Westgate Towers, and the former Holy Cross Church, can be seen in the background.

18. In the yard of the ancient St Mildred's Church a fallen tree rests against its more intact neighbour.

19. This tree which has blocked Castle Street fell from t former churchyard of St Mary de Castro, which is now pleasant open space.

20. Church Lane alongside St Mildred's Church provides convenient short cut from the Rheims Way to Stour Street. It i seen here strewn with torn off branches.

21. The aforementioned former church-yard suffered further tree loss and the way through was blocked for a number of days after the Hurricane.

22. This wholesale warehouse with part of its roof torn off, is seen here from the city walls.

3. Despite this scene of damage, the Dane John Gardens did ot fare too badly when compared to the Westgate Gardens or illers Field.

24. Back in the High Street the winds triggered many alarms and uprooted this tree in the small open space on the site of St Mary Bredman Church, demolished in the nineteenth century.

25. This small bridge carries a track from St Stephen's Road to Frank Hooker Field, over a branch of the River Stour. Debris from many fallen trees has caused the water level to rise, a contributory factor to the floods which were to follow.

26. A cityscape taken from the roof Telephone House in April 1987. T church in the foreground is St Mildred

27. This section of the Rheims Way was constructed in 1962, with an elevated section over the Westgate Gardens.

28. Looking into the city from t churchyard of St Martin's. The Cathedr can just be seen through the branches the huge Cedar of Lebanon.

. . . AND AFTER THE HURRICANE

9. Cityscape post Hurricane, taken almost a year to the day after photograph 26.

30. The devastation to the Westgate Gardens is graphically shown in this view, and the Tannery buildings can now be clearly seen.

The St Martin's Cedar is badly damaged, and a number of the small evergreens have perished altogether.

32 – 34.   This is the sad story of a single copper beech tree in th village of Bekesbourne. It must have stood its ground against th winds, as it was not uprooted like so many others, but eventuall torn off at the base.

35.   Other beech trees came to grief on that night, like these atop the hills on the outskirts of Bekesbourne and Patrixbourne.

36. The former railway station at Bishopsbourne is now a private dwelling. An array of trunks and branches have come down from the embankment and span the old platforms.

7. Just outside the village is Lenhall Farm, where these large evergreens have blocked the track to all but the most determined iker.

8. Bourne Park is a large area of parkland occupying the pace between Bishopsbourne and Bridge. In this area, many arge trees met their fate on the night of the Hurricane.

39. Down but not out. This tree, with some essential roots still connected, will probably continue to break into leaf in the due season, until it is cleared away.

40. The most common sight in Bourne Park today is chalk encrusted root balls standing next to their craters.

41. Bourne House can be seen in the distance between the fallen trees and the moody skies above.

42. Closer to the house is the impressive lake, which is fed by the stream known as the Nailbourne, which flows from its source at Etchinghill to its conclusion at Well Chapel, between Bekesbourne and Littlebourne.

43. These once fine examples have tipped into the waters of the lake, yet show signs of living on in the early spring sunshine.

44. This view of Bourne Park would not have been possible had this willow not been sadly mutilated. Despite the many losses, Bourne Park still has many fine outstanding trees, as can be seen here.

45. Taken in October 1986, this photograph shows the magnificent Cedars which stood guard on either side of the private road entrance to Bourne House.

46. A guardian no more. The Cedar on the left hand side of the road looking inwards was uprooted, like so many others on the chalky open areas in Kent.

47. The same scene as it existed in April 1988, showing the right hand Cedar which has survived, albeit badly damaged.

48. The solid chalk existing just below the top soil means that tree roots tend to spread out and along, rather than downwards, which may explain why so many large trees in this Park have been lifted out of the ground.

49. Sheep graze around the grouping of trees, some of which have survived, some not.

0. Nearer to Bridge now, and the scenes of damage continue. The tree top which protruded into the road has been lopped off, but the rest of it has been left where it fell.

51 – 53. A thin strip of mixed woodland existed along the lane just east of Bridge Church. Here both coniferous and deciduous trees alike have been uprooted. Some trunks rest against surviving trees, which are showing the first signs of new foliage. Others fell into the adjacent grazing land.

54. This photograph, taken just before Christmas 1986, features Bridge Church and the aforementioned woodland area.

55. April 1988, and countless destroyed trees, like this sad example, can still be found where they fell, some six months after their demise.

. This view, also taken in April 1988, atures the same scene as photograph 54, t with a vastly different skyline.

57. Renville Farm, near Bridge, was where this lofty specimen could be found. The farm track can be seen crossing a bridge of the former Elham Valley Railway Line.

58. This oak was carefully conserved when the embankment Bridge by-pass was constructed, in its shadow.

59. The country lane in this view, winding through the hamlet of Grays near Herne Bay, would take the traveller on to Marshside, Boyden Gate and Chislet.

). The Renville Farm tree is now as much a memory as the ains which passed under the bridge here, until the line closed in)47.

61. The severe lines of the by-pass bridge are no longer softened by the tree, whose torso lies along the bank of the Nail-bourne which trickles past here.

62. The lane at Grays passes through a much changed scene. The surviving tree in the foreground stands remote from the twisted wreckage behind it.

CHARTHAM HATCH (BIGBURY WOODS)

63. If you take the small road out of Chartham Hatch, towards Harbledown, then you will pass through Bigbury Woods.

64. Here, alongside the lane, a once proud row of evergreens have toppled over into the immature broadleaf coppice they once shielded from the passer-by.

65. In almost every case, the trees fell away from the road, displaying their brownish root balls, so different from the chalky masses found in Bourne Park.

66 – 68.   The fallen evergreens of Bigbury Woods when viewed in close-up, or at different angles, can create some fascinating and unusual studies.

HARBLEDOWN

69. High on a bank, above Harbledown by-pass and near where Palmer's Cross Hill descends from Rough Common, a massive evergreen tree came crashing down.

70. This huge dominating tree, seen by many people as they came into Canterbury, was sadly mourned when it fell from its high vantage point.

71. Other lesser trees in the vicinity also perished, as can be seen in this view. On the right, the by-pass turns away toward Canterbury.

72. Further along the same stretch of road could be found the now famous Harbledown Cedar of Lebanon, seen here in its full glory in the summer of 1986.

73. The Cedar survived the Hurricane but was so badly damaged that it was deemed unsafe and was felled shortly afterwards.

4. When the by-pass was built, the Cedar was retained on a specially constructed platform. This and the stump are all that remain. Damage to the nearby property caused by a descending Cedar limb is clearly evident.

23

75. Hillborough lies between Reculver and Beltinge, on the outskirts of Herne Bay. Being situated on high, open ground, it had very little protection from the Hurricane.

76. This farm building collapsed onto itself, but the rigid metal framework of the roof supports saved much of its contents from being crushed.

77. Another Hillborough building reduced to timber and rubble. The church of St Mary the Virgin can be seen in the background.

78. This view was to be found on the cross-country public footpath between Bekesbourne and Littlebourne, which made a much more interesting walk than the route by road.

79. A few days after the Hurricane, and much of the overgrown hedgerow has been torn off.

80. This photograph taken from the same position as in photograph 78 shows how much of the field could not be ploughed, because of the fallen branches.

81. This oast house can be seen at Preston Court, next to the lovely village church. Both buildings suffered damage to the roof, but the oast came off worst, being stripped of many of its valuable tiles.

82. This storage building at Lenhall Farm just outside Bishopsbourne, is being held up only by its contents.

83. A shed which was to be found on the lane between Herne Common and West Blean Woods has been reduced to so much firewood.

84. Sunday morning walkers survey this ruin in the tiny hamlet of Nash, near Ash.

85. This was once a woodman's hut, but its former shape can only be guessed at. It was to be found in Thornden Woods.

A collapsed shed on the road between Canterbury and Bekesbourne, a scene repeated many times across the county.

87. Over the last few years, the number of caravans at Reculver has been greatly reduced, as plans for more 'up market' recreations are being discussed.

88. The Hurricane reduced the numbers still further. There would appear to be little future for these two caravans locked together.

89. Another caravan has been flipped over onto its roof, causing the bodywork to buckle.

90. I took this photograph of Stodmarsh Church on a wet, wintry morning early in 1987, little realising how much of the scene would disappear later in the year.

91. On the edge of Stodmarsh these hilltop trees have fallen over in unison, towards the village.

92. Returning to the church, and the same scene as photograph 90, a year later. What better illustration of the change to our countryside wrought by the hurricane.

93 – 95. Another use was being sought for this redundant primary school on Sturry Hill, until a large tree in the grounds was brought down through the roof. Since then senseless vandalism has caused further damage and the whole structure has now been demolished.

96–98. A plantation of tall pines was to be found in Thornden Woods, on the road between Tyler Hill and Greenhill on the outskirts of Herne Bay. The mass of tall straight trunks resembled a forest of telegraph poles . . . that is, until 16th October 1987.

99 – 101. The comparison to telegraph poles now seems inappropriate when viewing the forest floor carpeted with debris. Those trees not brought down still lean over as if the Hurricane continued to rage through.

102. Thornden Woods before it all happened. This photograph looking back at the plantation was taken in May 1987, from the footpath that leads right through to West Blean Woods near Herne.

103. This view is from the road, and the damage is such that it appears as if a massive flail cutter had worked its way through the plantation.

104. Another view looking back at the plantation, taken in April 1988. The pine tree back drop has all but disappeared.

105 – 107. This was an overgrown plantation surrounding ponds and a spring, and marking the point where the Nailbourne concluded and the Little Stour commenced. The plantation was to be felled at the end of October 1987, and replanted with Ash. However, the Hurricane brought the trees down first, in its own devastating fashion.

108. This view was taken just three weeks before the Hurricane. The woodman can be seen in the distance, planning the felling operation.

109. Unfortunately an unplanned felling resulted, and with the surface so badly broken up, replanting in the immediate future now seems unlikely. The ruined chapel from which the area is named can be seen in the background.

110. Compare this view to the one in photograph 108 for the full effect of the devastation in this plantation.

111. On the outskirts of the village of Hoath is a hamlet called Old Tree. Old Tree House is seen here photographed on Thomas Becket day (29th December) 198

112. This is the Ford at Bridge, over which the Nailbourne trickles, and sometimes rushes, on its way to Patrixbourne.

113. Goodnestone Park is another area of parkland, like Bourne Park, which suffered significant tree loss. Goodnestone House is seen here within its walled garden.

. . . AND AFTER THE HURRICANE

14. Old Tree March 1988, and a umber of old trees have disappeared om the scene.

115. The area around Bridge Ford has been opened up by the winds raging across the nearby parkland. Note that the Nailbourne water level is very high.

6. Goodnestone House on a wet nday morning in March. The large ergreen has gone, and the nearby llection of Spanish Oaks show signs of uch clearance.

117. West Blean Woods is a large area of mixed wood and coppice land. Here a deciduous tree has been broken as if it was no more than a matchstick.

118. The Hurricane did not discriminate, and further into the woods an area of evergreens has been wrecked. Wellington boots are recommended when using the woodland tracks!

119. Here, the large fallen tree has also uprooted a coppiced stump, standing on top of its own rootball.

120. Neat ranks of deciduous and coniferous trees line the track, which has come all the way from Thornden Woods. This shot was taken in May 1987.

1. Previous coppice clearance had left a large open space, er which the winds raced, giving the exposed trees in this area y little chance.

22. This is the same view as photograph 120. The conifers ave gone, and the maturing deciduous coppice has been ravaged.

123. This is the village where a numb
of my ancestors lived and worked, abo
a hundred years ago. That is about ho
long these trees had stood on the green
Wickhambreaux.

124. The large house seen here was
featured in the film 'A Canterbury Tale',
which was filmed in the city and surrounding countryside during 1943.

125. This huge tree brought up a secti
of the road with it, and also demolishec
substantial garden wall on its way dow

6. The same fallen tree as was featured in photograph 125, t this view emphasises the size of the tree, and its rootball ich was over six feet in diameter.

127. This, and the view below, show just how much damage can be caused by one moderately sized falling tree. The top half is well embedded amongst the rafters.

128. The bottom half of the same tree has demolished this ancient wall. The middle section which spanned the road was quickly removed to open up communications.

129. This view of the green was taken in January 1987, just after the snows had cleared. The large tree in the centre of the picture looks immovable.

130. The same tree can be seen here up-ended. The concrete base on which the bench once stood was torn up at the same time.

131. The village green post-hurricane. The only consolation is a clearer view of the delightful St Andrew's Church.

2. Peter Docherty sits amongst the ruins of his garage, con-
ing himself with a coffee, having just dug his new car out of
rubble.

133. Tom Vine clears away the fallen branches of his weeping
willow tree.

134. The author risks life and limb to clear some precariously balanced tiles.
(Photograph by Sarah Brown)

AFTERMATH — THE FLOODS IN CANTERBURY

135. The water level in Canterbury rose dramatically after the Hurricane, and reached its highest point in January 1988 when this sequence of photographs was taken. This view is of Bingleys Island.

136. The River Stour divides into two through Canterbury, and with its various cross channels creates a total of seven islands. The minor branch of the river is seen here at Kingsmead.

137. The major branch of the Stour Kingsmead has broken its banks and flooded the adjacent nursery.

138. The Stour at Kingsmead further downstream. The bridge in the background takes Kingsmead Road over the river.

139. The design award winning supermarket is reflected on the floodwaters covering St John's Nursery. Plants poke their heads above the waters.

Looking towards St Radigund's h the Marlowe Theatre in the distance. river at this point is almost twice its mal breadth.

141. St Radigund's car park is awash and cars crowed into the greatly reduced space left above the water level. The former Frank Hooker School Annexe is seen in the background.

142. Looking along the Stour towards the site of Abbotts Mill, as the river rushes past. The banks and retaining walls along Solley's Orchard on the left have been swept away.

143. St Peter's Lane runs along the other side of Solley's Orchard. Flood waters from the nearby Stour bar the way. In this area sandbags were distributed to keep the waters out of the houses.

. St Radigund's Street runs over this bridge, and the Stour
ses beneath. Clearance has been reduced to practically
hing. When the water is at its normal level, remains of the
man city wall can be seen by the bridge on the left.

145. The flood relief channel at Millers Field comes into its
own at times like this. It is seen here at full capacity.

146. The relief channel passes under the Causeway to rejoin the Stour on the other
side. There is no more room under the bridge, and the water now rushes over the
top.

147. Barton Mill has been added to over several centuries, and is well worth seeking out; situated between Canterbury and Sturry, the mill looks down on the waters rushing past.

148. The Nailbourne flooded along its full length, and is s here just outside the village of Bridge.

149. The ford at Bridge usually carries a couple of inches of water. Here the Nailbourne has become so swollen that the ford is now too deep to traverse.